T0286000

GRAND TOUR

GRAND TOUR

FARRAR STRAUS GIROUX

POEMS

NEW YORK

ELISA GONZALEZ

Farrar, Straus and Giroux
120 Broadway, New York 10271

Library of Congress Cataloging-in-Publication Data
Names: Gonzalez, Elisa, 1989– author.
Title: Grand tour : poems / Elisa Gonzalez.
Description: First edition. | New York : Farrar, Straus and Giroux, 2023. |
    Includes bibliographical references.
Identifiers: LCCN 2023008714 | ISBN 9780374611378 (hardcover)
Subjects: LCGFT: Poetry.
Classification: LCC PS3607.O561325 G73 2023 | DDC 811/.6—
    dc23/eng/20230406
LC record available at https://lccn.loc.gov/2023008714

Designed by Crisis

Our books may be purchased in bulk for promotional, educational,
or business use. Please contact your local bookseller or the Macmillan
Corporate and Premium Sales Department at 1-800-221-7945, extension
5442, or by email at MacmillanSpecialMarkets@macmillan.com.

www.fsgbooks.com
www.twitter.com/fsgbooks
www.facebook.com/fsgbooks

3 5 7 9 10 8 6 4 2

FOR STEPHEN

After all, the good life
still is only: life

—Carlos Drummond de Andrade,
translated by Elizabeth Bishop

CONTENTS

NOTES TOWARD AN ELEGY

The Cypriot sun is impatient, a woman undressed
who can't spare the time to dress, so light
like a vitrine holds even a storm.
One day in the Old City, a pineapple rain.
And I'm on my way home from the pharmacy, carrying
    my little bag of cures.
Refuge at the café in the nameless square.
Nihal brings espresso poured over ice, turns off the music.
We listen to rain fall through the light until the end.

White wine greening in a glass.
Lion rampant in the sky. Moon reclined gorgeous in her silver shift.
Polished newels. Door askew in its frame.

Hot mornings. Hot apple tea, honeyed.
The mountains a fist knuckled on the horizon.
Dust is coming, dust is not yet here.

Whenever her hands dance, I tell her how beautiful.
She says there's so much other movement I do not perceive.
And I accept the presence of dances invisible to me.

Figs in the tree, figs on the stones.
Stains of rotting fruit spread and shadow at the sun's whim.

That steady dissolution of body into form that signals the progress
   of a masterpiece.

Copper bowl in her hands. In the bowl in the hands, olive leaves
   burn.

I ask her to read to me. I like the way her voice handles words.
What will she read? First she laughs.
It's a good day to laugh. The coffee is strong. And the light.
Why read when we can talk? When all our friends are here?

My perversity is silence, a shudder stopped
in the throat. When all the time I hear her voice:
I am glad my soul met your soul.

—Examples of what, I do not know. It's just that
for a time I took Love out walking
with me everywhere and sometimes I thought, Child, whose
   is this child?
when it played in the square. A sunshine creature, terrifying,
yet still I looked at it like I've never looked at a stranger
who promises water to the waterless for nothing.
And now I lie awake pretending everyone in the world
lies still the way the living are still:
not entirely, never entirely.

AFTER MY BROTHER'S DEATH,
I REFLECT ON THE *ILIAD*

The water cuts out while shampoo still clogs my hair.
The nurse who swabs my nose hopes I don't have the virus,
     it's a bitch.
The building across from the cemetery calls itself LIFE
     STORAGE.

My little brother was shot, I tell the barista who asks how things
     have been,
and tip extra for her inconvenience. We speak only
to the dead, someone tells me—to comfort, I assume, or inspire,

but I take it literally, as I am wont: even my *shut up* and *fuck* and
     let's cook tonight,
those are for you, Stephen. You won't come to me in my dreams,
so I must communicate by other avenues.

A friend sends an image from Cy Twombly's Fifty Days at Iliam
—a red bloom, the words "like a fire that consumes all
     before it"—
and asks: Have you seen this? It's at the Philadelphia Museum
     of Art.

If I have, I can't remember, though I did visit
with you, when you were eleven or twelve, when you tripped
silent alarm after silent alarm, skating out of each room

as guards jostled in, and I—though charged with keeping you
from trouble—joined the game, and the whole time we never
    laughed,
not till we were released into the grand air we couldn't touch
    and could.

You are dead at twenty-two. As I rinse dishes, fumble for keys,
    buy kale and radishes,
in my ear Priam repeats, I have kissed the hand of the man
    who killed my son.
Would I do that? I ask as I pass the store labeled SIGNS SIGNS.

I've studied the mug shot of the man who killed you; I can
    imagine his hands.
Of course I would. Each finger, even.
To hold your body again. And to resurrect you? Who knows
    what I am capable of.

If I were. Nights, I replay news footage: your blood on asphalt,
    sheen behind caution tape.
Homer's similes, I've been told, are holes cut in the cloth
    between the world of war
and another, more peaceful world. On rereading, I find even
    there, a man kills his neighbor.

6

"Let Achilles cut me down, / as soon as I have taken my son
   into my arms
and have satisfied my desire for grief"—this, my mind's
   new refrain
in the pharmacy queue, in the train's rattling frame.

The same friend and I discuss a line by Zbigniew Herbert
"where a distant fire is burning / like a page of the *Iliad*."
It's nearly an ontological question, my friend says, the instability
   of reference:

The fires in the pages of the poem, the literal page set afire.
We see double.
You are the boy in the museum. You are the body consumed, ash.

Alone in a London museum, I saw a watercolor of twin flames,
   one black, one a gauzy red,
only to learn the title is *Boats at Sea*. It's like how sometimes I forget
   you're gone.
But it's not like that, is it? Not at all. When in this world, similes
   carry us nowhere.

And now I see again the boy pelting through those galleries,
a boy not you, a flash of red, red, chasing, or being chased—
Or did I invent him? Mischief companion. Brother. Listen to me

plead for your life though even in the dream I know you're already
   dead.

How do I ensure my desire for grief is never satisfied? Was Priam's
   ever?
I tell my friend, I want the page itself to burn.

FAILED ESSAY ON PRIVILEGE

I came from something popularly known as "nothing"
and in the coming I got a lot.

My parents didn't speak money, didn't speak college.
Still—I went to Yale.

For a while I tried to condemn.
I wrote, Let me introduce you to evil.

Still, I was a guest there, I made myself at home.

And I know a fine shoe when I see one.
And I know to be sincerely sorry for those people's problems.

I know to want nothing more
than it would be so nice to have

and I confess I'll never hate what I've been given
as much as I wish I could.

Still I thought I of all people understood Aristotle: what is and
    isn't *the good life* . . .
because, I wrote, privilege is an aggressive form of amnesia . . .

I left a house with no heat. I left the habit of hunger. I left a room
I shared with seven brothers and sisters I also left.

Even the good is regrettable, or at least sometimes
should be regretted

yet to hate myself is not to absolve her.

I paid so much
for wisdom, and look at all of this, look at all I have—

ROMAN TRIPTYCH

I

Red stones piled in square towers.
Red roads cruise aqueducts.
Blue chain by the door
strikes a bell.

From our gold-draped room
the windows with their astragals and sashes
glass out the bottle-green hills.

I hold her naked on the carpet,
my body spilling
out of my lavender dress.

Body, if you could be forever
spilling out of your lavender dress.

II

Twin redheads fondle twin
Barbies, sliding sateen dresses

on and off the dolls' voluptuous physiques.
I tread on a grate and in a cloud
of vertiginous steam see in a store window my hands
disappearing under a mannequin's skirt.
The noise of a drill down the avenue
like whipped cream shooting from a can.

III

My hair tangles her fingers
till I unknot it, and I unknot it
as I've done many things
to detach myself
from pleasure.

She says the words I use remind her
that she is reading a poem,
referring to the above *vertiginous*—

Reader, I want you to know you are reading a poem.

What is the point of talking otherwise?

NOTES ON A DIVIDED ISLAND

Cyprus, 2018

I almost miss the taxi driver's words:

Do you love the sun?
If you will stay a long time, you must love the sun.
You will see. It shines 360 days a year here.

He hangs an eagle feather and a sachet of dried jasmine from
    the rearview mirror
so that when he looks behind
he has good luck.

My suitcase clops one-wheeled over stones.
In the house: a woodstove, a man feeding it.
I decline food.
I am somewhere between visitor and pilgrim, I haven't decided.

*

Muezzin competes with church bells.
One side of the wall, then the other.
A volley of worship.

I tip into day
through the prayer's bright holes.

*

In the life that develops,
a ginger cat dashes out the door after a gecko,
both soon lost in a convocation of petals.

I cross every morning.
South into North. In the evening, reverse.
Tendering my blue passport to the guards
on one side, then the guards on the other.

Have I ever before been ashamed of my ignorant courage?
Never to have feared a border or a crossing.

That first line slashed on a map in green ink by a general's pen.
And imagination sets a border unto today.

*

Above the mountains, a daring little plane.

Our shadows our cats they slip through cracks and of course
  they do.

History's pressures even under stress cannot be measured
like the diameter and elasticity of arterial walls.

Floods follow the old maps. Floods are rare.
(Draw your own conclusions.)

The sun shines only 300 to 340 days a year.
And though I've searched, I haven't seen the driver since.
In the end, would I reveal the brutal truth?

*

Shades come to life in the gloom of walls and mouths.
My mother and father don't belong here,
but then they have never behaved
according to any logic I understand.

*

It rains vakit vakit. It rains tekrar, tekrar, daima. It rains bu sabah.
    Başka bir şey yoktur.

I am horribly in love. When we take shelter under a balcony, I say,
We could be each other's great tragedies had the world not slaked
    us already:

A sea generous with plastic, more and more; a wall from the sea
    to itself again.

He compliments my wisdom.

                                    *

Whatever I take in my arms, I look like I am selling something.

The rainy weather will leave the country at four o'clock,
the newspaper prophesies in Greek.

After the rain:

Hast thou money? asks a man spraying a pink wall with his pee.
It is absent, I say

but he looks at my face suspiciously, and it's like when I pry skin
from a fig with my fingernail to see it curl and give.

                                    *

On this island the sun works
hard as the mother of hardheaded children
who repeats, Look what you did. Just look.

See, my mother *is* here.

*

The square I visit morning after morning
has no name and no postcode
because the number-giver hasn't come.
If in bureaucracy we live, are we dead here?
The dead drink coffee then.

*

Every word I speak is followed by a lesser one.
I'm a visitor who's overstayed enough to pretend a life.

What might I leave behind besides a little dimensional disorder—
    that my body will stay after I go?

At that café in the square I linger with my book, half-drunk
    lemonade puddling the table
in an image on Google Maps.
Dusty white shoes and a denim dress. Unfinished book. Title
    obscured.

A stranger set me there. Another stranger showed me.
Uploaded and I didn't sense.

I didn't know my hair was so long or so dark
but I know the distance I cover
without moving.

TO MY
THIRTY-YEAR-OLD SELF

In two years, you'll forget
how old you are, subtract

a year from yourself.
That's age. That's

hope. Someone will correct
this error. You'll hate them.

You excel at hating, you excel
at untrammeled feelings,

mostly ugly, though also
generosity, and sacrifice

which can, at times, make
ugly things happen. I'm afraid

I can't explain why you failed
your younger versions,

just as I've failed you
when we all agreed

on the great project
of our life: to write well—

not *well*, I can hear you thinking,
to write *perfectly*. If I answer

That's impossible, that was never possible,
you'll turn away, enraged

at your own mind. Another
nightmare. After another.

It's like you're my sister.
I still cherish you.

A woman so relentless
in stupidity and pursuit.

Like a dumb dog. Like you
at twelve, and two, and twenty-one.

Remember writing that first story?
It was terrible. Immediately

you wrote another.
That's hope. I think I remember.

We were six.
We had no judgment, only promise.

FABLE

In the spring, ducks kick through reeds
spreading shore to shore on the unnamed pond.
The air reeks of ducks and thick, propagating reeds.
The children in the house like to watch
from the window, though they turn afraid
when the ducks flock. Ducks nip at ankles and toes.
The mother and father let the reeds grow
without objection, and the pond greens and stinks
in the sweaty parts of summer
when no one wants to be outside.
Sometimes the father takes a gun off the wall
and goes out to shoot at the ducks
or the deer that come close to the house
in the dregs of winter
as if they know something about what's inside
and what could be given to them:
apple cores, hard cracked corn aplenty.
The deer stare into the windows.
It makes the children sad,
the same way the ducks' dying makes them cry.
But once, for Easter, their father gave them a pet duck
and they didn't take care of it.
You see the problem: what does it matter if he shoots

at the air, or the duck, or the deer
when the air is grayed like strands of hair
and the children will cry in any case
simply because they are children?

TORNADO IN AUGUST

Disasters are coming to us
here, but we don't acknowledge this ever,
my mother and I. I talk about God
while she hangs up fresh⁄washed linens
and delicate items to dry. Her pale pink brassieres swing
open like the breasts of women nursing children.
She has many children, of whom I am the oldest,
stricken now with a harsh cough
and the guilt that comes from knowing my mother
is drying clothes for me that I no longer wear
only put in the laundry every two weeks or so
just so she thinks I like that sweater
and now those white sweaters and white sheets
hung out on the line spin because the drying tree spins
as I used to spin. And everything
is as I used to do.

A TUESDAY IN MAY

My grandmother died the day
the missionaries came for our souls.
To save them, I mean.

They cycled up the drive
as my mother and I carried her to the van,
on our way to the hospital.

We didn't hear them till they dismounted,
we were so bent on moving her
without pain.

Their hands waved hello.
There was nothing
for the bicycles to do,

so I looked at the wheels
not the missionaries, who asked,
Do you have a source of happiness in your life?

What was my answer, what is it now?
My grandmother swayed
like a hammock between us, then stilled.

They sprang to help.
Bicycles clattered on asphalt—
Did we use dogwood switches? Did we use stones?

SONG OF EXPERIENCE

Though I had the pocket-sized rage of a child too old for tantrums, it feels untrue to say I was so *miserable*. I had devil eyebrows when my mother French-braided my hair, skin yanked taut. I matched my hair ribbons to my sisters'. That was all fun. Fun, too, was the lion poster on the wall of my Sunday school room, where I savored grape juice in Dixie cups, palmed goldfish crackers snacked on during the boring stories, all of Jesus, whom I pictured blank as an uncolored figure in coloring books. I was an angel one year, then the king bearing myrrh. That was when I was very young. But the year I turned seven I saw many fearful things. My father died on the cross, waist wrapped in a sheet my mother hadn't wanted to surrender. His head lolled on his shoulder. The centurion, Mr. Garza, gored his side. I was punished later for disturbing the service, for running up to touch his feet, for wailing—It was my father's performance, interrupted before resurrection, and after that I think it's safe to say I was not *innocent* anymore.

EPISTEMOLOGY OF THE SHOWER

We were thirteen. R explained that her parents forbade her
    showering alone
because she had been masturbating. She didn't use that word.

I was lying on a blow-up mattress beside her bed. Our habit
on Saturday nights, so together we could rise at seven and ready
    ourselves for church.

This was why I would have to shower with her in the morning.
    A masturbation monitor.
Each of us, she quoted, has a habitual sin.

To offer some sin in return, I said, I think I might be a lesbian.
    I'd never met one
as far as I knew. I knew the word, I thought I knew what it
    signified.

How do you know? she asked, and through the dark I could
    hear her terror for my soul.
I retracted: Maybe I'm wrong. Maybe I just hate men.

My habitual sin, we already knew, was hating
my father, whose habitual sin was hitting me. Through
    the dark, R reached for my hand.

I was nineteen when I concluded that I *was* wrong, that the word
     I needed—
insofar as a word confines desire—was *bisexual*, whose sound
     I loathe. No music.

But at this party there's music:
a Greek song loud as in the center of the room a man dances
     the zeibekiko.

Wild cheers as he circles and circles a glass of red wine. To finish,
     he falls
to his knees, picks up the glass with his teeth, tilts his head back.

I dated that man for a while, I've seen him dance this dance.
Tonight I miss the finale. I'm out in the stairwell

kissing A, whose long auburn hair preserves my modesty
as bliss destroys thought.

But the next morning, in an unfamiliar bed, I do think of R's
     question, answerable
only by the body—like, I'd argue, faith, the faith that habitually
     tumbled the two of us

to the sanctuary floor, overcome by the Spirit. She kept her faith.
She grew up to be a godly woman; I racked up habitual sins. I
     desired, desire

such knowledge from this world that if age one day empties
    my mind
I sometimes think I'd be grateful. Imagination, too,

is old habit, assiduously maintained
despite consequences. For instance, I can easily imagine
    damnation, as I did in R's room,

my hand in hers. The usual visions of hell. Then the shock of sun,
    the shock of cold water;
some boiler problem. We showered anyway, together as
    commanded. Shivering, wet, we

slid our hands across each other's bodies for warmth, ostensibly.
One pretext leads to another:

I pretend not to understand the shower's workings
so that A will help, and then join, and then and then and then—

I learned you can separate pleasure from disgrace, though
it's hard to make a habit of pure happiness, when there's so much
    to know.

This morning even before
I drew back the curtains I felt the smog
in my nose and chest,
a strong smog layering light
in the sky, tessellating yellow
and pink like a ballerina's tulle,
a beauty not consolation
but misdirection, because
we go on abiding and abiding
the source of it:
we light coal in the fireplace
on cold nights, open the chimney
so the sky is the one
adorned by smoke
like the smoke I used
to mark my arrival home,
a little yellow house
beside the paper factory.
My sulfurous youth.

my brother gets out of bed at three, having lain down
only a few hours before, and pulls on his jeans, and stubs his toe
   on the doorjamb,
and cuts himself, just a scratch, reaching too fast in the dark

for wallet and keys—and the weapon? A bill, probably.
He goes out under the huge sky, out of the small house
and beyond, fields upon fields, where as children we played
   hide-and-seek and tag

and all those games, I miss them. All we imagined. In my
   brother's mind
the fuzziness of the awakened-too-soon after not-enough-sleep
and the resentful calm that comes

when doing your duty to those you love,
to whom you could not
do otherwise.

He drives too fast, as always, braking hard when he finally
   arrives
at the meadow my car slid into before it slid
into an oak

where a whitetail hangs, strung
by its hind legs to drain the slit throat.
It takes more time than I expected

for death to be over,
I tell my brother. And he, a hunter, says, Yeah
in the tone that means, Of course.

And years later I have the same voice
when he calls at 4:17 a.m. and I knock the phone off the bed,
answering almost upside-down, stretched toward him.

His pain then, I lived for it, I realize now.
Not for its existence, but to quiet with my words.
I had left so long ago. I had left.

The doe's eyeshine keeps us company. We joke
about our dead new friend. We share a fifth
of Jim Beam tugged from under the passenger seat.

By the time the tow truck rumbles up, it's well into dawn.
We are giddy—like children
who have played a game so wholly they have forgotten

the rules of the real world, and naturally
don't want to remember. My brother turns to me near sunrise
to ask, What do you think he's doing? Right now?

And I spin a story of a father
waking to polish his teeth, spit blood
into the eye of a porcelain bowl, wash a face like my brother's.

That was a game, yes, us seeking the man
he was when not hurting us one and then the other,
and then the game ended

as children's games do, when authority says
it's time to disperse,
when the other gets on a plane, and one is left.

CYPRUS

A rare thunderstorm.
Bougainvillea riots outside the window.
Rain's blue diamonds. A stunted lemon tree.

Then a series of words replete with definition.
Just yesterday, I still believed I could tell the story
someone else longed for. It's rained twice in a month—miracle,
    people say.

I came to this island begging for everything.
A classic error of love—yes, I am aware—
to be convinced one knows what the word encloses.

Yesterday, cursing his children, the neighbor
cut down branch after branch of trumpet flowers.
They fell on our side of the wall.

Osmosis. Xylem. Mesophyll.
So the water rises.
And there go the blossoms, panicking across the garden.

SECRET AND INVISIBLE
FOLDS INTO THE VISIBLE

after Augustine

Lately I have been lullabying myself to sleep with erotic fantasies.
Familiar vision: my psychiatrist pins me against the wall of his
office. Gold lotus print I recognize from the Met trembles beside
my head. Calendar shakes, too, over his shoulder. It's January. As
I pass into dreaming, a woman pushes me into a bathroom stall
to reveal the black bootlace dangling from my vagina. This is how
they control you, she whispers into me, and presses the aglet's tip
with a manicured thumb. The Editor would delete all of this,
would save me from my propensity to humiliate myself. But I have
a young man's mind, deranged with desire.

FIRST MONTH IN NICOSIA

In our dreams starlings fly roundelays
above a city of ruins and tumble down
down into invisible trees
confused but alive.

Out of the dust blots at first
what seems a starling
what *is* a drone—
ah here in these streets seven hundred years old
the disappointments of modernity patrol.

Someone is shouting, What do you know? What do *you* even know?

IT TOOK DOMINION EVERYWHERE

after Wallace Stevens

The shoe man tells the carob man to tell the tea woman to stop making such noise when she boils water. The kettle's toothless whistle disrupts the tick and whir of his sewing machine. You take my hand when we approach the crossing at night, and—this is the sign—keep hold after we're through. The silhouettes who slide from the wall live otherwise as cypresses, nightjars on the wind. No one questions the line we cross. Where we walk next, our shadows raging under streetlights, our animals as hungry for dailiness as passion, every noise and calamity of love.

AN ARRANGEMENT
OF THE BEGINNING

The priest
chants vespers in Polish, doors thrown
wide and oozing godlight into the street.

Startling at each other's touch.
Such pent‑up electric joy
as if a younger self.

Rain. Flight from rain.
Rain in the eyes.
On the hands touching other hands.

If there was anything to say,
for once I refused.
Dark covering over half her face.

WHAT HAPPENS

when a snake is born to a woman?

Tacitus (Book XIV of the *Annals*, A.D. 109) offers:

"There occurred too a thick succession of portents, which meant
nothing. A woman gave birth to a snake, and another was killed
by a thunderbolt in her husband's embrace. Then the sun was
suddenly darkened and the fourteen districts of the city were struck
by lightning."

He moves on.
Blue apparitions of citizens
rush to quell the lightning.

Which meant nothing.
A thick succession of portents.
Many things would be explained if
we could know our real genealogies—

Why did I leave loyalty's elegant rooms?

Today, after breakfast, on my wrist,
kitchen burn like a cabochon ruby
returns me to the stained-glass glow of a classroom

where a switch-thin professor explains
that in Petrarch love is three.
The lover requires a lover
looming beyond
the beloved
in order to love.

In an eye, in a mirror—

The mastery of passion requires loneliness.
The teacher said.

Whether *touch me* is dictum or query
hinges entirely on how it is marked
out by small dots.

But I am losing the grammar.

It was autumn, it was a sudden thing.
I introduced the Third Person.

TO MY
TWENTY-FOUR-YEAR-OLD SELF

Sometimes you feel more intimacy with the woman who lives
in the apartment opposite—twenty years older, probably,
though she looks barely ten, devoted to evading age—
than with anyone stroked or kissed or otherwise handled.

You sit naked on the white sofa, lights on, looking into her home,
    lights on.

She paints her toenails, watches a black-and-white film,
Hitchcock, maybe: there's a woman with a platinum chignon.
She applies a green mask. A cream. A mystery ointment.

When you meet an older woman who resembles her, enough,
you do the obvious thing.

That woman says, after, Don't ever leave me
but when you report to your friends
you change her words to Don't ever forget me.

Typical of us, the lie and the lie.

Why couldn't you tell the truth? That's what I've come to ask.
Not to her—to your friends.
I can't remember why it embarrassed you.

Was it that she was old enough not to bare her throat?
Or was it shame at yourself, for misunderstanding
how well you were understood?

(It always comes back to knowledge with us, doesn't it?)

Maybe it doesn't matter: you'll think of this woman
so often throughout the years
that by some lights

you'll have kept your vow.

THE AORIST

When I set this mouth of mine to talk talk talk
I've undone it. Poor tongue
gathering scraps of Turkish
to speak with you.

Your English says, When there was not
the two of us this hand
of mine still
reached for you.

Use this tense,
my textbook directs,
only when an action is
neither past nor present nor future.

I think, What freedom,
until I learn that only habit comes untied
from time. When we spend ourselves every morning

in the same bed. When we practice.
To kiss, to go down, to come.
To stroke. To lift. To stray. To laugh.
To sleep, and of course to take, to give.

Yet you still don't know
where this hand of mine has traveled,
and I know when I touch
myself no one gives me anything—

How to tell you, The urge to run comes
from time to time?
Your morning murmur: I'll put the coffee on.
Why tell me, when you always do?

When messenger wind alarms the shutters.
When jasmine whirls through the gap.
When I rise. When I dress.
When I shut. When I goodbye.

PUENTE DE PIEDRA

Cabo Rojo, Puerto Rico

Wearing white to make of myself a friend to those who haunt the sunlight, I clamber down limestone steps to a crescent of stones, a beach made by the waves rolling and breaking in patterns governed by forces you may know intimately now, if you have survived death—

What can I describe that you have not seen (if you do see)?

A philosopher tells me that I am thinking of everything in the wrong way: what is *survive* what is *death* what

If he means to stump me, it can't work: *to survive* is to wake up early and for a period no longer than twenty to sixty seconds not remember that you are dead.

To survive is to pray this interstice repeats every morning for the rest of my otherwise unendurable life.

And death? (I smile enigmatically)
Death to philosophers! What do you think of *that?*
(He disappears, mosquito in the bladed breeze.)

This bridge of stone is natural. In specifying, I realize that most bridges are unnatural, so to speak, and I would like a substitute word unspoiled by human structures, if you have one in a language that perhaps you now know, even if every word will sound like wind to me.

I could learn the names of all the winds, at least.
Even alive, I could.

An arch from cliffside into the sea, through which the sea

through which the sea—

a portal to where the dead survive, I am describing to you, I understand now—which you have already recognized from the other side. I am waving. I am waving from the shore. I am dressed in white. From your vantage can you see if you do see how others who have come here, living or dead I do not presume to guess, have made piles of stones in white and pink and umber and the exact shade of a mountain riverbed, and interspersed among the stones also white, whorled coral, dead?

If I pass under the bridge, what then? Do you answer in the wind or the waves or the stone or the silence? Do you care? Do you care to answer?

Scraping the stones on the seabed with my fingers, as far down as I can go, eyes closed—

How this particular dark is or could be like surviving death, where everything you can't see is what you touch.

Tonight, as perhaps you know though I do not yet, I will ascend a bridge of stars that are in fact fluorescent lights strung at intervals according to an engineer's logic, to prevent some dying, on my way to the other side of the island. Surviving,

a young boy gathering stones and shells to show me, one after another described as if I couldn't see—I didn't—the wondrous characteristics for which you chose these among all the world, and these treasures, like me, unaware.

And death—

Were I just a little quicker to turn my head, might I see you there, in form perhaps something like the changeable blue no one living can describe, certainly not me? This language I do not have yet.

SUNSET

A trampled carnation, or the red jacket sleeve
blurred on that girl quickening
after the ball

draws my mind
to the ship that I am told
is coming, preparing to anchor.

I am turned toward the sea.
It pauses at the bay's red mouth:
When everyone seems so happy, why does it delay?

IV

THE ICE STORM

felled the hawthorn.
All furred in crystal, everywhere
the extravagant declaration of ice.

Over the carcass roamed
my ungloved palm.
My tender, curious fingers.

Nevertheless,
in the months that passed,
the earth warmed.

The neighbors inquired politely
if I would ever get rid of that dead tree,
it was an eyesore, really a menace.

I didn't oil the chain saw, I didn't hack away
the crown of branches.
Refusal, my life.

Occasionally I dreamed of a bonfire.
Like Savonarola, I concluded
the only way to purify was to burn.

Lighter fluid. Limbs woven
over kindling. I could see it.
The possibility of a brilliant end.

My chapped hands laid
a circle of stones
to witch the flames.

But a wet spring came upon us,
and my dreams went dark,
after which I learned there are several methods

for disposing of the dead.

IN QUARANTINE, I REFLECT
ON THE DEATH OF OPHELIA

I wake early and angry, I eat oatmeal with thyme honey,
I call my sister, I call my mother, I call my other sisters,
    my brothers,
I worry about my coughing lover, I worry about my siblings,
    jobless now.
I send an ill-advised email, I don't send an ill-advised text.

I'm alone so I'm lonely. That's what my sister says.

Time to stay indoors, the doctor says, all the doctors say,
but the open window betrays that not everyone's voice dies to
    solitude.
Shut up, shut up! the window slams.
Time to embrace the virtues of boredom, the price of happiness
    again, after.

The window shows men digging a place for survivors of
    the future, the rich ones.
It will be a condo tower, glass walls for better envy.
They've built the frames, I see, around the holes where doors will
    someday go.
Capitalism! So full of holes and hope.

If I try to remember what it was like, childhood, a period of
    kudzu
growth that *felt* like stasis in the white-glazed room where days
    upon days my father shut me—
if I try, I see the ceiling, that water stain trailing down
like brown Pre-Raphaelite curls, hair of a drowning girl among
    reeds,
which later I recognized in a painting of a pale drowning
    Ophelia.

I love alone, I tell my sister. She says, You just want to.

I agree I want the past.
For a magnolia to bloom on a crowded street, all safe in beauty,
    for I
still love the world, though it drowns
and dies like that girl, avoidably.

A professor once asked, pleased we wouldn't know,
Who is really responsible for the death of Ophelia?
The answer, he said, ought to feel like we have arrived together
at a skyscraper's peak, where the inhuman
view reveals in windows and in streets
the small, sick or potentially sick bodies—each one a new array
    of questions.

The only possible epiphany is that the ending of a thought is
    never such.

Together. I liked the word in the professor's mouth.

But if I am alone, and if I am lonely, and if I am not alone in
　　loneliness, and if the everyone

together suffers, and if this everyone suffers and dies by the
　　unguided motion of matter, and if

also by the motion of selfbent self-guided men, and if also by the
　　motion of money, and if of course

you were always going to die, Ophelia, and if even so your death
　　remains unforgivable,

then what questions should I ask? All I have is sleeplessness
　　and rage,

and that's no answer, it's not even a thought, though it might not
　　end till my body does,

perhaps not even then, as I can imagine it going on past my
　　ending, and really—

what more suitable ghost could I leave behind? Since I do love
　　the world.

TRAVELING SHOW

The apartment of a Croatian couple, husband and wife, both
 in love
with our friend M, a professional flautist, long-fingered and
 heron-legged.
They've gone to Zagreb to witness a mother's death.
For the duration, my husband and I walk their mutt, Streetboy,
 in Tempelhof Field.
My husband hates Streetboy. Streetboy retaliates. Streetboy pees
 on our pillows. I forgive Streetboy
without hesitation. I pity Streetboy as I pity anyone entrusted
 to my care. If I were virtuous,
Streetboy's bladder would last the five flights and three blocks
 to Tempelhof.
My husband reminisces about when he lived here a decade ago.
 One winter dark
so insistently that on the first day of real spring sun, he wept.
Yet, he maintains, he was happy then. He keeps describing
 happiness
as Streetboy lunges for a bicycle and almost dies, which
 wouldn't
have been my fault, truly, however much it felt like it.

All my husband's happiness lives in the past. And this, the
    afterlife?
Paradise is a club in Mitte where I've never danced.
The couple returns. They pay in drugs for our trouble. It turns
    out
it was the husband's mother. It turns out Streetboy's name is
    Stribor.
How apt! I think. A shared hallucination of a name is a good
    description of marriage.
But it means surprisingly little to set word to action. If you even
    manage it.
Like: Once, in Manhattan, we slid dollar-store rings onto ring
    fingers
as the officiant barked, Look at each other! Don't you know what
    you're doing? Okay, *now* say it.

WARSAW

An apartment whose six windows overlook a courtyard polluted
    with crows
against whom the residents wage war. Their infantry? Realistic
    simulacra. Metal murders
perched on balconies. Blank iron eyes. Awake when I wake to the
    morning's gray hours.
By lunch, the fake crows look ludicrous.
I mock their sentinel stares. I take the side of reality.

My husband talks about the evolution and peculiarities
of Corvidae, these oscine passerine birds. They're so smart—
crows one of the few animals, counting humans, with object
    permanence.
The drama of crow versus sham crow acquires novelistic
    proportions.
In the evenings, we read novels in separate rooms
or in the same room and it makes no difference,
a compression that would interest me if it were someone else's
    loneliness—
thoughts I'd once have mentioned, at least, to the man in the chair
    opposite,
my husband it seems, who is subsiding, who does subside
into his mind over the course of a long, smogged winter, the air
    sometimes so toxic we cancel
drinks with friends for the sake of everyone's lungs, though he still
    smokes and we still drink.
In fact, we even discover vodka! Albeit poured in small goblets
    and sipped.
When we do go out, it's to a bar called In the Fumes of the
    Absurd, if translated literally,
where I reject the symbolism I still reject.

ON THE NIGHT TRAIN
FROM GDAŃSK

before I learn that in Kraków someone I love did not
    kill himself
because I am on the night train from Gdańsk, I wander
    carriages hunting an open seat, at last
settling for the corridor's cold floor. It's a cold October outside
    this rumbling and screaming
contraption, where I'm quick to shift aside for the blond nun
    I disappoint
by saying, No, I don't know where the toilet is or if it has paper,
    and where I jump up
at the conductor's brusque Pani, proszę. He cups his hand like
    my father beckoning for me
to surrender whatever small thing I loved, but this man needs
    a second-class ticket to validate
my seat on the floor, my back against the cold wall, my hair
    tangled on a screw.
On my knees I prop *The Selfishness of Others*. Przepraszam,
    I say to everyone angry
at my body's inconvenience, everyone who passes, including
    the nun, who returns
rubbing germs between her palms. Forgive me, that I have
    a body—a thought I've had many times.

My father, who hated my body, asks me to stand—no, it's the
    conductor talking, again,
as if we're new to each other, as I've greeted people whose
    nakedness I regret touching. Forgive
the weakness of the mind confronting the shames of the body.
I thank the conductor, I cover my face with *The Selfishness*
    of Others, I close my eyes.
This is before. I am telling a story of before. Before I learned to
    purchase first-class tickets,
to choose trains from this millennium, not this creaking and
    wailing artifact
where an old woman raps the conductor's shin with her cane as
    she berates him for the lurch, the crush,
assigning him sole responsibility for all of Poland's trains, which
    he refuses.
Forgive me for the sins of others—that's not something people
    say if they can help it.
This is before again. Before the nun disembarking at a town
    I recall only as fluorescence
and the screech of brakes gives me her window seat, for nothing
    I have done.
The world becomes perfect in its repetition of vanishing: flash
    of light, then dark, again and again,
signs of people I'll never meet. Many years before I arrived
    in Poland
I pictured myself wandering alone, away from my father's
    house, not realizing

—I was a child, and children are the most hopeful narcissists—
that wandering happens alongside others. What else didn't I
    know? That I would love
places glimpsed through dirty glass, that now fondly I think of
    the couple splitting
a ham sandwich, mayonnaise-smeared, beside me, and how
    suspiciously they regarded my hands.
That I'd love that stupid sandwich; the dry, overheated air; the
    blushing ugliness of faces, such as mine.
The window's chill against my cheek—even that, despite its
    comfort.
The conductor who once again checks my ticket. When I was
    young, I believed that one loves only
what deserves love. Forgive me, Father, I said, that I am hateful.
    Glow of towns with names invisible
passed by in a wheezing and roaring beast. Memory of childhood
    is a history of error—
so I think on the night train from Gdańsk to Kraków, believing
    I am experienced enough
in the daedal web of selfishness and love to pack the book away.
    Forgive me,
he said, for even thinking about it. I thought about it before I
    thought about you finding my dead body.
What else could I do but thank him? What else don't I know I've
    been spared?
By others, by the faults of memory . . . The conductor taps my
    shoulder and the sandwich-eaters

call out in Polish then English to wake me: Przepraszam, this is
    your station.
Down the platform a dark-haired stranger approaches, listening
to her own music. Ticket in hand. Did she take my place?
    I've wondered since.
I wondered—forgive me—even as he was talking, confessing
    as much as he thought I could bear.

TO MY

THIRTEEN-YEAR-OLD SELF

I know how tired you are
of dreaming your father's death.

If the two of you live as duelists,
as you've long thought,

then if one dies, the other
has killed. Most of the time

you believe it will be you
who ends it, and have prepared for the consequences,

dreamed those out, too: the arrest,
trial, foreclosed life—and judged

it a good sacrifice, if it spares the ones whose faces appear
when, awakened from a world in which you are generous

and grant him a pleasant death,
you close your eyes again.

Your brothers, your sisters. Your mother.
And you, alone in your head—

you prepare your courtroom speech,
a splendid oration. I'm sorry

you will never tell them what
we both know. I know in other dreams

he kills you. And I know you have girded yourself
not to plead. You intend to die a Greek hero.

You've made notes on the *Iliad*.
I remember the lines.

When you're older—eighteen or nineteen—a teacher will say
casually, as if commenting on a superficial quality,

Your hate is utterly fearless. I know
you spot the error in this statement.

Then a dreamless night, though not
restful at all, and in the frayed

morning, you'll know what I know
to be true, and hard, and a blow, and a blessing, maybe:

that his death when it happens (it hasn't
yet) may have nothing to do with you,

that you trained yourself to a purpose
for nothing. Sometimes it really is for nothing

that you have to live. What is it you dream,
apart from him? If I remember correctly:

even then, the whirling
of peregrinations, elsewheres, a chaos of faraway—

Never do we learn to sleep well, unfortunately,
but you'll sleep badly, or not sleep,

and sometimes dream little easily forgotten tales,
in many beds, beside many bodies,

and, with the alertness of the thoroughly exhausted, walk
    new streets
fearless or fearful, it doesn't matter—the point is,

you say to the teacher, that no action
depends on feeling. It was *will*.

And anyway (you'll misquote)
still the girl dies

who has done nothing
as the man who has done much.

HOME

I

Mama sings of the sea when she does laundry,
or she sings old hymns she learned in West Virginia.
So God washes up onshore the color of sand,
smelling of clean clothes. And the songs keep us company
in the mornings, and in the evenings
when we carry it all inside.

II

When Mama plants a magnolia,
I become a gatherer of magnolia stories.
A ruthless explorer with mahogany carrying cases
for biological specimens, a thousand flower presses, a gun.

Linnaeus named *Magnolia virginiana*,
more commonly sweet bay magnolia.
Sweet bay, Mama loves the name.

Sweet bay,
the exact pink of an old teacup,

the underbelly of a secretive jungle bird
found at long last, taken dead
into the hold of a dank ship.

III

A face behind a sunflower,
grass-stained legs, dirt-digging thumbs
counting off age: 1, 2—
Mama takes the photo.

Later I plant peonies. My sister plants hydrangeas.
The house gets smaller because the plants get bigger.

We hide in the garden before he comes home.
After, my sister cleans off Mama's feet, I clean off her face.

Mama lets the magnolia die. The lilies,
frail orchids, the petunias sturdy in the window boxes—
all brown and droop. She tends
unblooming shrubs: seasonless, green.

When we leave in the night, Mama forgets to bring
the flowers and even the herbs.
In the new house we have long grass, untended.
In the fall, a yard of unraked leaves.

IV

Mama sobs as she soaps the dishes.
Through the window, the backyard grows
indistinct. It fades
into green points, darker green swirls.

Mama in bed all day: I only want to sleep.
I want to sleep forever. Why won't you sleep forever?
Why won't you let me sleep?

In my dreams, I stand between her body and a black wave.

Wake up, wake up!
To everything that's sad, I can add something happy . . .
The color of the water—I promise it isn't black, it's a pure
    unwasted yellow.
And the sun will come alive.
And the boats will come, too, circling under the sun.

LOVERS' DISCOURSE

Where you were not born
but brought as a child,
high on a mountain
that is also a volcano,
you were surrounded by fog.

I like the idea of a world of clouds
and so I want to watch you
walk down to the sea as you used to
from the mountain's peak,
descending into the sun,
fog like cobwebs in your hair.

Once, when you were four
or seven, before you were first sad
and after you were first angry,
you went to a petting zoo.
A goat bit you.
You tried to bite the goat back.

Now, turning to me in bed, you say
that was the only time you were happy
and I interpret this to mean

you were scared, or defiant.
Which isn't true.
That is, the only time you were happy
before you were happy with me.

AN ARRANGEMENT OF THE END

Ah, there: the space on the floorboards
where you sat braced
against the white wall,
face averted from the window, the streetlight,
and my face, streaked
with occasional siren reds and blues.
To see oneself as if not oneself, to obscure the other—

Across the street, a woman pauses so a bulldog can appraise
a heap of dirt. Down the block, sounds of a revival,
the preacher chanting hallelujahs.

You get up to go. Tomorrow he'll travel on.
How many revivals should one life contain?
After all, I searched years for a room like this,
and at first I strode around like a child, proclaiming,
Here is the bed. Here is the window. Here is the door.

You admired everything I named. You caught
my hand when I pointed at something I can't picture now,
though for an instant I must have loved it, too.

THE MOUNTAIN LION

ate the girl
when she went alone
to the outhouse at night.

The black grass rustled, the black leaves,
the lion in the trees
leaped. Someone screamed—an owl.

Dark everywhere in the forest.
Then from the lighted house,
gunfire, late.

(She didn't tell her father,
who held the rifle,
that she was leaving.)

Everyone will try to keep you always
but it's all right to go to the forest and the animal,
if you really want.

MIRROR

I offer a friend's young daughter a leaf
of mint just picked, inviting her to smell,
when the past alights

and that other garden run amok
envelops. I am
overgrown.

Crush of mint
under the heel of a little girl
enjoying her small but definite powers.

Rain last night, caught in a black bowl.
Inside, a face flickers. Whose?
Espejo, my friend instructs. Espejo de agua.

I water the herbs
though it galls, this encouragement
of any future.

Now the girl names all the plants she knows.

Now the wind sweeps away the debris.

Now she asks, ¿Qué has visto?

PRESENT WONDERS

That morning light from two large uncurtained windows
    doesn't correct.
My sleepy eyes. They stay small, stupid and grumpy.
That nonetheless the rest of me moves.
That it's accident, but the light and I touch my desk at the same
    time.
That the light doesn't have hands. It seems like it should. It draws
    shapes the way hands do.

That I'm not dreaming, because in dreams I can never
talk, and today my mouth is so dry I try infant sounds for
    elemental needs: wah for water, et cetera.

That my fingers miss the keys.

That suffering is often speechless, sometimes soundless, and yet
    we understand it exists in the absence, too.
And yet have I ever not been shocked at pain? Like a toddler
    falling down.

That there's no elegy for the ongoing.
When elegy travels from lament to solace, to return us from grief
    to life, to strip us from the dead.

Not yet. Not yet.
To honor suffering when honor puts gravestones where no body is,
    hides bodies where no gravestones are.

Well, I can't.

That I used to speak as a whole being without doubt. Or do I
    misremember.
I tend to brighten the past, shadow the present—which is
    shadowed, don't mistake.

That I am angry though powerless, like a child.

Well then today I am a child.
And with a child's voice deepened by some form of progress,
    I ask for water.
The same cadence, the same intonations—insistent and afraid
because all lack in childhood feels forever: a fever thirst, a mother
leaving for her job at the grocery store, a door locked to keep you
    safe.
Small fists against the cold door.

That they didn't break it down, that they bled, that they hurt only
    later and now, not in a dream but in silence,
a pain like light against a wall, or just against.

/

The epigraph is taken from "A Mesa" ("The Table") by Carlos Drum-mond de Andrade, translated from the Portuguese by Elizabeth Bishop.

"After My Brother's Death, I Reflect on the *Iliad*" includes quotations from the *Iliad*, translated from the Greek by Stanley Lombardo, and "Trzy wiersze z pamięci" ("Three Poems by Heart"), by Zbigniew Herbert, translated from the Polish by John and Bogdana Carpenter. *Boats at Sea* is a watercolor by J. M. W. Turner.

"Roman Triptych" is also the title of a poem by Pope John Paul II.

"Secret and Invisible Folds into the Visible" is a phrase from *The City of God*, Book XXII, Chapter 24, by Augustine of Hippo, translated from the Latin by Marcus Dods.

"It Took Dominion Everywhere" is a line from "Anecdote of the Jar," by Wallace Stevens.

"What Happens" includes a quotation from the *Annals* of Tacitus, as it appears in *The Complete Works of Tacitus*, translated from the Latin by Alfred John Church and William Jackson Brodribb.

"In Quarantine, I Reflect on the Death of Ophelia" includes a reference to the painting *Ophelia*, by John Everett Millais. The phrase "unguided motion of matter" is drawn from writing by Cotton Mather on the New England earthquake of 1727. "Selfbent" is, as far as I know, a word coined by Gerard Manley Hopkins in "Ribblesdale."

"On the Night Train from Gdańsk" refers to *The Selfishness of Others*, by Kristin Dombek.

Both "Home" and "The Mountain Lion" have been set to music by Stephen Feigenbaum and have been performed by ensembles such as SACRA/PROFANA and the Boston Children's Choir.

ACKNOWLEDGMENTS

Thank you to the publications in which some of the poems in this collection first appeared, often in slightly different form and in some cases under different titles:

American Chordata, "Epistemology of the Shower"

Barrow Street, "Tornado in August"

Cosmonauts Avenue, "Roman Triptych"

Foundry Journal, "First Month in Nicosia"

Harper's Magazine, "Mirror"

The Minnesota Review, "The Ice Storm"

Mississippi Review, "The Aorist"

The New Yorker, "Notes Toward an Elegy," "After My Brother's Death, I Reflect on the *Iliad*," "Failed Essay on Privilege," "A Tuesday in May," and "In Quarantine, I Reflect on the Death of Ophelia"

Palimpsest, "What Happens"

The Paris Review, "Traveling Show" and an excerpt from "Notes on a Divided Island"

Prelude, "Weather Journal, Warsaw," "An Arrangement of the Beginning," and "An Arrangement of the End"

Tin House, "Secret and Invisible Folds into the Visible"

*

Thank you to my editor, Jonathan Galassi, for knowing just what to question in a line.

To Louise Glück for more than I can say. Your unwavering belief in my poetry, and in this book, kept me writing even when I had none.

To Jameson Fitzpatrick, who reads every draft of every draft, for being my co-conspirator in life and literature; to Carina del Valle Schorske for an ongoing exchange that is all gift, no debt; to Hannah Aizenman and Lauren Roberts, whose insight shaped many of these lines, for years of entwined creation; to Laura Marris, who read some of these poems when we were so young we had no idea what we would become, for helping me become a poet; and to Maggie Millner for much-needed encouragement when I faltered near the end.

To Deborah Landau for pushing me toward wildness; to Edward Hirsch for unstinting generosity beyond anything I deserve; to Anne Carson and Robert Currie for making me less afraid; and to the entire New York University creative writing program for the freedom to discover.

To Paul Yuckman and John Faulkner for teaching me how to really read poetry. To Andre Willis for teaching me to read Aristotle and to question whatever I am taught.

To Gabrielle Bates, Caroline Beimford, Jamel Brinkley, Nicole Cecilia Delgado, Stephen Feigenbaum, Sara Freeman, Bean Gilsdorf, Rainer Hamilton, Marwa Helal, Patrycja Humienik, Kamran Javadizadeh, Shawn and Joshua Liu, Kyle Carrero Lopez, Ricardo Maldonado, Grace Needlman, Sarah Nutman, Mara Pastor, Alicja Rosé, Monica

Sok, and David Wingrave for conversations that enlarge my sense of this art's possibilities and never, ever bore me.

To Hannah Wilentz for helping me title this book.

To Simon Bahçeli for making me feel golden, and to so many in Cyprus—especially Beran, Michael, Yeliz—for sharing the island with me.

To my brilliant agent, Alice Whitwham, for understanding me in all genres.

To the Rona Jaffe Foundation, American Academy of Arts and Letters, U.S. Fulbright program, Rolex Foundation, Bread Loaf Writers' Conference, Kingsley Trust Association (especially James K. Robertson), and Center for Fiction Writers' Studio for crucial support.

To my mother and siblings—Traci, Melissa, Micaela, Caryl, Olivia, Julio, Gabriel, Stephen, Miguel, Chanah—for a love that sets the measure of love. You were my first readers. You are my dearest readers. Everything I write originates in you.

Not a word in this book can be severed from its dedication.